Are you excited about planning your next trip?

Do you want to try something new?

Would you like some guidance from a local?

If you answered yes to any of these questions, then this Greater Than a Tourist book is for you.

Greater Than a Tourist- Dallas Texas USA by Blaise Ramsay offers the inside scoop on Dallas. Most travel books tell you how to travel like a tourist. Although there is nothing wrong with that, as part of the Greater Than a Tourist series, this book will give you travel tips from someone who has lived at your next travel destination.

In these pages, you will discover advice that will help you throughout your stay. This book will not tell you exact addresses or store hours but instead will give you excitement and knowledge from a local that you may not find in other smaller print travel books.

Travel like a local. Slow down, stay in one place, and get to know the people and the culture. By the time you finish this book, you will be eager and prepared to travel to your next destination.

>TOURIST

IF FOUND PLEASE RETURN TO:

👤 _____

✉ _____

📱 _____

GREATER THAN A TOURIST BOOK SERIES
REVIEWS FROM READERS

I think the series is wonderful and beneficial for tourists to get information before visiting the city.

-Seckin Zumbul, Izmir Turkey

I am a world traveler who has read many trip guides but this one really made a difference for me. I would call it a heartfelt creation of a local guide expert instead of just a guide.

-Susy, Isla Holbox, Mexico

New to the area like me, this is a must have!

-Joe, Bloomington, USA

This is a good series that gets down to it when looking for things to do at your destination without having to read a novel for just a few ideas.

-Rachel, Monterey, USA

Good information to have to plan my trip to this destination.

-Pennie Farrell, Mexico

Great ideas for a port day.

-Mary Martin USA

Aptly titled, you won't just be a tourist after reading this book. You'll be greater than a tourist!

-Alan Warner, Grand Rapids, USA

Even though I only have three days to spend in San Miguel in an upcoming visit, I will use the author's suggestions to guide some of my time there. An easy read - with chapters named to guide me in directions I want to go.

-Robert Catapano, USA

Great insights from a local perspective! Useful information and a very good value!

-Sarah, USA

This series provides an in-depth experience through the eyes of a local. Reading these series will help you to travel the city in with confidence and it'll make your journey a unique one.

-Andrew Teoh, Ipoh, Malaysia

>TOURIST

GREATER THAN A TOURIST – DALLAS TEXAS USA

50 Travel Tips from a Local

Blaise Ramsay

Greater Than a Tourist- Dallas Texas USA Copyright © 2018 by CZYK Publishing LLC. All Rights Reserved.

All rights reserved. No part of this book may be reproduced in any form or by any electronic or mechanical means including information storage and retrieval systems, without permission in writing from the author. The only exception is by a reviewer, who may quote short excerpts in a review.

Cover designed by: Ivana Stamenkovic
Cover Image: https://pixabay.com/en/dallas-texas-city-cities-urban-1740681

Greater Than a Tourist
Visit our website at www.GreaterThanaTourist.com

Lock Haven, PA
All rights reserved.

ISBN: 9781983209697

>TOURIST

50 TRAVEL TIPS FROM A LOCAL

TABLE OF CONTENTS

1. Howdy Ya'll
2. Of Airplanes and Trade Centers
3. Where Will I Stay? Depends...Where're You Goin'
4. Hope You Like Skyscrapers
5. I'm A Dallas Cowboys/ Mavericks Fan
6. It's Not The Heat, It's The Humidity
7. Yes, We Have Starbucks
8. Need A Way Around
9. Be Sure To Check Out Fort Worth
10. Get Social...Apps you Might Need
11. Master the Mix Master
12. Historic Grapevine, City of Wine
13. We're Still Country
14. Fishing, Hunting, and Lake Love
15. Be Careful After Dark
16. Cross The Crosswalks Correctly
17. Don't Mess With Texas
18. Things To Eat
19. High Five the High Five
20. Right Side of The Road
21. Need A Translator?
22. Best Time to Visit
23. Ripley's Believe It or Not

24. Medieval Times
25. Visit The Arts
26. Stop In at the Perot
27. Best Shuttles & Buses
28. Ride the Train
29. See Six Flags Over Texas
30. Best Grocery Stops
31. Vegan and Organic Foods
32. International Food Stores
33. Worthwhile Stops
34. Seasonal Sensations
35. Local Malls
36. Outlet Malls
37. Best Camp Sites
38. It's A Speed Limit, Not A Speed Suggestion
39. Be Safe When Driving
40. Times to Avoid the Roads
41. Weather Habits
42. Arlington
43. Local Colleges
44. The Grassy Knoll
45. The Kennedy Museum
46. Legoland
47. Sea Life
48. The Dallas World Aquarium
49. The Arboretum

50. Bonnie and Clyde Days
TOP REASONS TO BOOK THIS TRIP
50 THINGS TO KNOW ABOUT PACKING LIGHT FOR TRAVEL
Packing and Planning Tips

DEDICATION

This book is dedicated to those who love to travel and explore new places. To all the fellow Texans who call Dallas their home. To lovers of barbecue, country music and fried chicken. Most of all to the men and women in uniform who give everything so we can enjoy them.

ABOUT THE AUTHOR

Blaise Ramsay has been a native Texan for her whole life. A southern gal at heart, she has a love for everything related to the Lonestar state. She lived in Augusta, Georgia for her husband's military service but the call of the Lonestar drew both of them back to their home state. A lover of country music, open kettle grilling and summer nights, Blaise loves nothing more than to watch her children play around in the front yard while steaks are sizzling.

When she's not working in building her publishing company, FyreSyde Publishing, offering marketing and Scrivener coaching to indie and self-published authors, Blaise likes to stay at home in her small home town of Pilot Point, TX. Home of Bonnie and Clyde lying just north of Dallas! She enjoys a nice cup of coffee and some quiet time after the kids go to sleep to write or catch up on her rather long reading list.

HOW TO USE THIS BOOK

The Greater Than a Tourist book series was written by someone who has lived in an area for over three months. The goal of this book is to help travelers either dream or experience different locations by providing opinions from a local. The author has made suggestions based on their own experiences. Please do your own research before traveling to the area in case the suggested places are unavailable.

FROM THE PUBLISHER

Traveling can be one of the most important parts of a person's life. The anticipation and memories that you have are some of the best. As a publisher of the Greater Than a Tourist book series, as well as the popular 50 Things to Know book series, we strive to help you learn about new places, spark your imagination, and inspire you. Wherever you are and whatever you do I wish you safe, fun, and inspiring travel.

Lisa Rusczyk Ed. D.
CZYK Publishing

OUR STORY

Traveling is a passion of the "Greater than a Tourist" series creator. Lisa studied abroad in college, and for their honeymoon Lisa and her husband toured Europe. During her travels to Malta, an older man tried to give her some advice based on his own experience living on the island since he was a young boy. She was not sure if she should talk to the stranger but was interested in his advice. When traveling to some places she was wary to talk to locals because she was afraid that they weren't being genuine. Through her travels, Lisa learned how much locals had to share with tourists. Lisa created the "Greater Than a Tourist" book series to help connect people with locals. A topic that locals are very passionate about sharing.

>TOURIST

WELCOME TO
> TOURIST

>TOURIST

"Texas isn't just a place on a map... It's an idea in the hearts of our people."

– George P. Bush

1. HOWDY YA'LL

Congratulations! You are one lucky person. Why? Because you have just stepped on the soil of Texas. Dallas is one of the largest cities in the state and a bustling hub of business, leisure and exploration. It is a city full of things to do an see. It's the place I've called home for the last 31 years of my life and the birthplace of my business, FyreSyde Publishing. Odds are you probably if you arrived via plane you touched down at DFW Airport. In and of itself, DFW is a place of amazing exploration. There's a Chili's there that my family and I stop in almost every time we fly. It's huge and holds multiple shops to help you learn and get a first glimpse of Texas pride. You might find tons with the Texas flag and our state animal, the Armadillo with a cowboy hat on. We display it proudly! The best part, many of the people who work there are pretty willing to help so don't be afraid to approach either them or a local for some tips on where to eat or stay. We might even run into each other in because I do book events around the Dallas/Fort Worth area. Feel free to stop by any say hello. We don't call it southern hospitality for nothing!

2. OF AIRPLANES AND TRADE CENTERS

Not from around here? Overseas visitor? No problem! You have but to walk around the airport and find a way to get a hold of a few US Dollars. Something fun to know is Dallas and Fort Worth are trade centers. There are many different forms of currency exchanging hands. Dallas is listed as one of the busiest trade centers in the US. If you need to exchange some foreign dollars and cents, be sure to seek out the currency exchange centers. If there isn't one in the airport (which I'm sure there is) then there is one lying just outside of it! Again, we're usually pretty friendly so don't be afraid to ask!

>TOURIST

3. WHERE WILL I STAY? DEPENDS...WHERE'RE YOU GOIN'

Depending on what part of the metroplex you're staying at, you can find any number of five star hotels. Dallas is a business center. It houses many different trades who need to stay in high-end hotels. There's the Hilton, Double Tree, Omni. The list goes on. Personally, I prefer the Double Trees. They have some of the best continental breakfasts and are conveniently located near almost every event I attend. The employees are really kind and tend to give cookies. One time they gave my husband and I at least ten of the cookies because we were leaving late in the evening to avoid the crazy traffic. (More on that later) If you're looking for more modest pricing, we have that too. Often, the hotels listed above will offer a variety of different venues depending on your needs. Doube tree let us stay on the second floor for a modest price. The view was great! We could see the lights of the city perfectly. Of course, there's always websites like Travelocity or Kayak where you can search your local area. Personally I like to map out the rooms and take advantage of the early bird specials depending on the event I'm set to attend at the time. Don't have a smartphone? Don't worry. We have computer cafes as well! A little tip, if you enjoy conventions revolving around anime, costuming, etc then check out the hotel schedules. They may have some upcoming events during the time you've chosen to visit. As I've mentioned, I love to attend them to meet new and potential readers. They are great places to find handmade crafts, books, comics, etc. The vendors are very kind and the hotel employees often offer help.

4. HOPE YOU LIKE SKYSCRAPERS

Dallas is a skyscraper city. The buildings in and of themselves are beyond beautiful and well worth a look. Especially at night. Finding a good spot to park at a local parking garage was always a favorite hobby of mine. There was often a cool breeze and the lights and sounds of the city were relaxing. Various business and popular names can be found both inside the Metroplex and around it. For example, have you ever heard of iStation? Odds are your children have used its programs in their education. My sister works there and my kids use the program at their school. They loved hearing their aunt worked at the very place they use. Amazon and Toyota are two other well-known names who call Dallas home. The Big Ball as I call it is known as Union Tower. It is actually an eatery that slowly spins (don't worry, you can't feel it). I actually ate there. Stepping out on the balcony gives you a perfect view. It's often hard to not imagine Spidermand or Batman sitting at the very tops of them. The city at night is a glorious spectacle of lights and sounds. There's never a moment when something isn't going on. The American Airlines center is popular for well-known names like Lady Gaga and Justin Timberlake. If you're into names like Travis Tritt, Luke Bryant or Toby Keith, Billy Bob's is a good place for you to look. Some of the biggest names in country music perform there and it's rare they aren't traveling into town.

5. I'M A DALLAS COWBOYS/ MAVERICKS FAN

If you are from out of state and are an avid sports fan, then most likely you have heard of the Dallas Cowboys football team and the Dallas Mavericks basketball team. If this is you then I highly recommend heading over to Frisco, TX. The new Star center is the brand new building where the Dallas

Cowboys do their field training. The Mavericks (home team of Dirk Nowitzki) can be seen playing at the American Airlines center. Both have players who live in the local area and can be seen if you look in the right places. Many of them actually live in Frisco and the surrounding areas where they practice! Something to note, however, is that some of us, myself included actually aren't fans of either team. For example, I'm actually a New England Patriots supporter. It's always funny to see the reactions of people who aren't from the Metroplex when you mention you aren't a fan of the Mavs or the Boys as we call them.

6. IT'S NOT THE HEAT, IT'S THE HUMIDITY

Depending on the time of your visit, Texas can get hot! Dallas is a fully concrete and building city so it can feel like an oven. If you're visiting any of the metroplex cities, be sure to carry water. Not doing so can be dangerous, believe me. You never know when a case of heat exhaustion can hit. Wear some sunscreen and find a nice place to hang out inside during the day. What makes it feel so stifling is the water in the air. Texas used to be a dry heat state but here recently, it's changed. I lived in Georgia and thought the humidity was horrible. When I left Texas was a nice dry heat. When I got back, it was beyond suffocating. If you're finding you're having a hard time once you step into the summer sun just know, it's not the heat, it's the humidity! Good thing we have plenty of places you can pull the boat out and take a dip in the lake if you need to cool off.

7. YES, WE HAVE STARBUCKS

Due to its high traffic, Dallas is a very caffeinated city. There are no shortages of where you can get coffee or tea for those times you need to cool off or just want a place to hang out and meet people. You can find a Starbucks on every corner (almost literally). If you're most of a mom and pop coffee shopper, we have those too. Might need to leave the city to the smaller outlying areas to find them though. Who knows, you might get lucky and find a donut shop or Dunkin Donuts! I used to work there and heard from various customers it's actually new the DFW area or the South in general. I am a big fan of Dunkin's coffee and would recommend their Butter Pecan to anyone who was looking for good quality coffee and didn't want to spend a small fortune.

8. NEED A WAY AROUND

If you're new to the area and didn't bring your vehicle, it's no problem. There are many different ways to get around in Dallas. For those who are app users, there's Lyft and Uber. Friendly drivers offer their services to taxi you around to where you want to go. This is a great way to find regular transportation. Taxi and shuttle services are also available if you're more comfortable with those. Then you can always rent a car for a reasonable prices. Super Shuttle is one my family used when we needed to get to the airport on our way to Florida. The shuttle arrived right on time for us to get to our flight and was there when we got home to take us back. I was too young to remember how much it was but what I do know is they are still one of the most widely used bus around here. Yellow Cab is another helpful cab service my mother in law liked to use for her mother. The driver was very kind and waited for them to get her groceries to and from the house.

>TOURIST

9. BE SURE TO CHECK OUT FORT WORTH

Fort Worth is what we here like to call our sister city. Like Dallas, Fort Worth is bustling with activity. There are many different variations of activities to fit your specific needs. Nightlife? No problem, check out Billy Bob's or the Stockyards! Family? There's the Fort Worth Zoo and the Water Gardens. Racing fan? Why not drop by Texas Motor Speedway? Believe me, it's worth looking into.

10. GET SOCIAL...APPS YOU MIGHT NEED

Social media that is! By now, you've looking around at some of the sites and found a place to stay, yes? Well, Dallas is an avid user of all kinds of social media. We love the selfie as much as any other Texas native. Shoot some photos and hashtags and see who responds. It's a great way to meet new people! In the recent Superbowl, the kid known as "selfie kid" started trending on Twitter! Never know what may happen! Some popular apps you might want to look into are Lyft, Uber, Grubhub, Google Maps and perhaps Groupon for those who want to save some money while they're shopping around for things to do. There are a variety of deal on RetailMeNot as well.

11. MASTER THE MIX MASTER

Ah, the Mix Master. One of the most notorious high rises in Dallas. So often a local will be asked where the Mix Master is. If you're planning on staying in Dallas, you must master the Mix Master. It is a tangle of high rises that can get you almost anywhere. It may appear to be nothing more than a series of roads and overpasses but believe me, it's so much more. One year while at a convention, a personal friend asked me to take her to see the legendary Mix Master. When we arrived, she actually started to snap pictures and wanted me to take her over a couple of the overpasses. Every single time we got to the top, she would stare in awe at how far it stood off of the ground. This is actually a common reaction for folks seeing it for the first time.

>TOURIST

12. HISTORIC GRAPEVINE, CITY OF WINE

Stop a Dallas native on the street and ask what other sites to check out, they're going to say Grapevine. This city houses one of the most beautiful and historic downtown districts in North Texas. A wonderful place for wine connoisseurs and sight seers alike. Be sure when you're there to check out Gaylord Texan and Great Wolf Lodge! During the holidays, I tend to bring the kids out to see the giant sculptures of different characters like Shrek, Donkey and Fiona from Shrek or Anna, Sven, Olaf and Elsa from Frozen. During the year they had Kung Fu Panda, the kids went down the ice slides. We also got go into a small theater to watch Puss In Boots on a big screen. I actually danced with the person in the Puss costume. So many photos went up on Facebook for family and friends to laugh at.

13. WE'RE STILL COUNTRY

Other than Billy Bob's and a few other places, you might not see too much of the "country life" in the city. Good thing is all you have to do is travel a little farther north to Sherman and Celina! Celina hosts

Cajun Days, a whole dedicated to country music and creole cooking. Not to mention the drive is full of rolling hills and farmland! There's still hints of country but it ain't in the city. Most of the hills are on the outskirts and they are a sight to behold. Sometimes while on my way to events for work, I like to stop and take photos of the different seas of green, cattle and farms that litter the hill country. Being a small town girl, myself, I often take great pleasure in seeing these beautiful spectacles. Heading down to San Antonio is beyond beautiful. There's often nothing but land as far as you can see. No gas stations for miles so if you're planning on traveling long distances of country road, make sure you either fill up or have a spare can of gas.

14. FISHING, HUNTING, AND LAKE LOVE

If you're into living the outdoor life, there are a quite a few lakes and marinas that rent out their boats for people who love the lake life. Designated areas for hunting depending on the time of season are available as well. Cities like Pilot Point offer hunting and fishing licenses for the hunters and lake lovers looking to have a good time out on Lake Ray

Roberts! You can even go RVing! Some outdoor places to mention to get some really quality supplies are Dick's Sporting Goods, Outdoor World or Bass Pro Shop are some good places to start. Bass Pro and Outdoor World are two of my favorite places to go in and look around. They're huge and often have a set-up where the hunters who own the store set up their trophies. These are good places for photo opportunities.

15. BE CAREFUL AFTER DARK

While most of us are friendly and willing to help our fellow man. Dallas does have its dangers. Be very sure you don't travel late at night by yourself. It is unfortunate but sometimes it's better to be safe than sorry. Texas is now an open carry state so if you have a license you are permitted to carry. However, it isn't advised to go against the requests of the local businesses. My mom has the right to carry a concealed weapon. There are two places I would recommend avoiding after dark: Lover's Lane and Harry Hines. These streets are notorious for missing persons and local crime. Avoid them if you can.

16. CROSS THE CROSSWALKS CORRECTLY

In Dallas, the traffic can get pretty wild. Follow all the road rules. Cross only at the crosswalk when they tell you to cross. It may be tempting to jay walk when things look quiet. Don't. Use those buttons and listen for when the crosswalk tells you to go. Yes, they do talk here! Even so, it is likely you will get the last minute gunners who like to try and beat the red. Make absolutely sure you're clear. In Frisco, I have the hardest time getting to Starbucks because of the cars speeding through. This is in a parking lot! Imagine if you were trying to cross the middle of the road at rush hour. Whatever you do, make sure you are crossing safely.

17. DON'T MESS WITH TEXAS

Dallas is a very well-known party city but we respect the way it looks and often don't take kindly to messy streets or trouble-makers. We do have southern hospitality and stand beside each other but respect around here is mutual. Just remember the Golden Rule and we should be able to get along just fine. I know myself, I will go behind a local who decides to litter and pick up after them to keep the streets from being messed up. With the ever growing development, many of our cities strive to make their area appealing to prospective homeowners and buyers. Don't throw your cigarettes out of your window. You can and will get in some trouble.

18. THINGS TO EAT

There are many places to eat in Dallas of all kinds of foods. If you're into barbecue and brew, check out one of the local breweries. They're some of the best places to get steaks. Texas Roadhouse is a staple and can be found along many major highways. You can have peanuts and throw the shells right onto the floor. One of my absolute favorite places to eat is Chilis. It has a variety of everything! You can get sizzling fajitas, juicy hamburgers, baby back ribs and one of the best margaritas I've ever had. It's called El Presidente and it is still my favorite in any other place I've eaten. Another place I enjoy is Red Lobster. Every year on my birthday, I get taken to eat there. If you like some of the most amazing seafood and some great cheddar biscuits, stop in! To this day, I go to Red Lobster. Last but certainly not least, I love Cajun and Creole foods. No other place serves them better than Razzoos. At first glance, it seems a bit crazy on the outside but don't let it fool you. They make some of the best gator this side of the Mason Dixon Line. My favorite though is the crawfish. Deliciously buttery and juicy to the taste. For an experience, check out Genghis Grill! You choose your ingredients and fit it into a single bowl. They cook it all up for you and deliver it straight to your table!

19. HIGH FIVE THE HIGH FIVE

Like the Mix Master, the High Five is an icon to the Dallas area. One simply has to turn on the radio to hear its name either before or after work hour traffic. The news of traffic stops and wrecks may not always be pleasant but the High Five is still well-known to Dallas and its inhabitants. For a visitor, driving over it will definitely be an experience no matter where you're heading. Remember the friend I mentioned who wanted me to drive the Mix Master? Well she also wanted to see the High Five and go over it. Once again, she had her phone out taking pictures. Funny thing was, she was from Benbrook, Texas. Only a three hour drive away. Seems it's not only visitors who want to see it but Texas natives as well.

>TOURIST

20. RIGHT SIDE OF THE ROAD

For an international traveler, it may be strange to have the steering wheel on the left and having to stay on the right side of the road. I would recommend having someone drive you at first so you can get used to it. Dallas traffic can be dangerous if one doesn't know how to navigate its winding roads and sudden changes. Otherwise, feel free to grab a cab or shuttle or simply ride the train!

21. NEED A TRANSLATOR?

No problem at all. Many local business in Dallas and the outlying areas employ translators for non-native speakers. We are a city rich with all kinds and we like to make it as easy as possible for folks to get around. Don't be shy, we usually will help find someone who can help. For example, my husband works with folks from all walks of life. Some of his customers require him to call on an employee who can speak a different language and he's more than happy to get them to help. He usually he says he never wants a customer to suffer for being different. Just another example of southern hospitality at work.

22. BEST TIME TO VISIT

Honestly, there is no best or worse time to visit. Seasonal events occur during Halloween, Thanksgiving and Christmas like Holiday in the Park or Fright Fest. Otherwise, doing some research into the weather patterns and temperatures may help benefit you in packing proper clothing. Always carry an umbrella and Bermuda shorts and you should be fine as we like to say.

23. RIPLEY'S BELIEVE IT OR NOT

If you travel in Dallas, Ripley's Believe It or Not and the Palace of Wax have to be on your itinerary. Both places are full of wild facts, videos, wax figures and displays you have to see to believe. The outside of the building alone can be enough to draw you in! It's unbelievable! This was another destination I used to frequent for my birthday. I was always fascinated by some of the oddities I saw in the many videos. To give an example, did you know there was tornado so strong it threw an envelope through a telephone pole? A cow was thrown from a full-fledged twister and landed on a hay bale and survived. Just some of the wildest stuff you would never believe. The Palace of Wax had some of the most realistic figures I've ever seen. Clark Gable looked like he could come to life at any minute!

24. MEDIEVAL TIMES

Right across the freeway from Ripley's is a building resembling a medieval castle. This is Medieval Times. It is another very popular attraction. Once you walk through the doors, across a moat, you are taken back in time where swords and sorcery clashed with kings and queens of the realm. You are assigned a knight whose strength in battle is measured by the amount of cheering you give them. It is a fun experience for any level of visitor. My sister used to go here every year for her birthday. She loved the Red and Yellow Knight and even received a flower from him one year. I'd never seen her turn so red.

25. VISIT THE ARTS

The Arts district is downtown. You can find the Kimbell Art Museum and the Dallas Museum of Art where you can enjoy some traditional painting and design. The Music Hall is located in Fair Park and is a perfect place to enjoy live action theater where multiple awards have been given to many of its shows. There are many students who frequent the museums. Why? Because the Art Institute of Dallas is located only a few miles away. When I was in college and took Art History, we had to go to either the Kimball or the Dallas Art Museum to study the paintings and write short reports on them.

26. STOP IN AT THE PEROT

The Perot is a very popular science building. It contains various scientific and natural exhibits safe for the whole family. At certain times during the year, you can find a great dinosaur exhibit or summer camps for when the kids are out of school. You can also book birthday parties, weddings and other events. Definitely worth a look for visitors.

>TOURIST

27. BEST SHUTTLES & BUSES

There are a variety of bus and shuttle services in Dallas. Dart and Super Bus are two highly used services but they are not the only ones. Echo and Charter are two other services you can look into if you wish to price match. If you do not wish to use any of the local bus services there are also many of us who use Uber and Lyft.

28. RIDE THE TRAIN

Recently Dallas opened up what is known as the Dart train. It runs not only through Dallas but also down Central Expressway and up into Fort Worth. It's an ever expanding mode of transportation that can get you to many different places or as close to your destination as possible. Be careful at night. It can be tempting not to watch the rails late at night but always play it safe.

29. SEE SIX FLAGS OVER TEXAS

One of the most well-known and popular attractions near Dallas is Six Flags Over Texas. It is a huge park full of fun rides, games and roller coasters for anyone in the family. If you prefer water parks for those hot days in the summer, that's no problem. Right across the freeway is Hurricane Harbor. It is a wet and wild world of fun with popular rides like the Black Hole. For those who come during Halloween, there's Fright Fest or Holiday in the Park for the Holidays. Both are a must see at least once!

30. BEST GROCERY STOPS

Of course, there's going to be the time you might need to grab something quick for the road. Well, for that there are many different stores you can go to in order to get a hold of clothing, food and snacks. Target and Wal-Mart are two of the most well-known and hold clothing as well as food. For quick food runs, you can find a Kroger, Tom Thumb, Aldi and Market Street. Whatever your needs, no matter how fast or slow your stay, it won't be hard to find what it is you're looking for. Market Street and Whole Foods are two of my favorite places to go. They offer a wide variety of Non-GMO and Organic fruits and vegetables. I used to work there in the seafood department and found a love for the Steelhead Trout. If you're ever in Market Street, grab a filet. It's a delicious, sustainable fish. Much more buttery than salmon and lacking the fishy taste. Whole Foods has a brand of pickle that is great for your stomach. They're called Bubbies and they are fermented rather than made by the old pickling method. I eat one of these after each meal and don't have to worry about bloating or upset stomachs.

31. VEGAN AND ORGANIC FOODS

Are you vegan? All Organic? Non-GMO? We have that too! Market Street, Whole Foods, World Market and yes, even Wal-Mart have a variety of goods for those watching their health and what is in their food. Often these places are open late or are open all day and night long. There are many locations around the Metroplex. Often hotels will have brochures to show you where to go to find them.

32. INTERNATIONAL FOOD STORES

Aside from Market Streets, Whole Foods and World Market, there are specialty stores that carry different ethnic foods. For example, if you're really craving some authentic Latin or Hispanic cuisine, La Fiesta is a good place to go. For Middle Eastern or Indian Foods, there's India Bizarre or the Patel Brothers. These two places are pretty awesome to step into and have a wide selection. If you're interested in a sit-in restaurant for Asian food, the Little Sheep Hot Pot in Plano, just south of Dallas is great. A pot of broth is brought out along with a menu for you to choose your own meat and vegetables. There are three rounds and the best part, the mochi! This sweet potato treat is delicious and goes great with the meat meal. Beni-Hana's is another Asian cuisine place I would recommend to anyone. It is located in Dallas and is made in the form of a Shinto shrine with a koi pond and everything. Some of the cooks do flips with their spatulas and tricks with the food that is not only entertaining, it leaves you wondering how they do it.

33. WORTHWHILE STOPS

Some worthwhile stops that may be smaller are the Gearbox building in Frisco, Texas, the Dallas Public Library or the Union Tower. They are all interesting places because Gearbox is a well-known company responsible for producing big name games such as

Borderlands. This is currently my favorite place in Frisco. Borderlands is my absolute favorite video game that isn't on PC. To have one of the hubs of the company that makes it in my backyard is beyond amazing. Attached to Gearbox is a café dedicated to those who work at Gearbox and folks who enjoy video games in general. During the holidays, the square is lit up with a fascinating display of dancing lights. Folks come from all around to see it. It's a stop my family makes multiple times every year. Our kids just love it! The Dallas Public library is massive and sports many different books on multiple subjects. Union Tower, as mentioned before, is one of our most popular landmarks. Even if you aren't wanting to eat, standing on the balcony and looking out over the city at night would be worth the time. There's also the Mobile Tower which sports the red Pegasus that lights up on New Year's Eve.

34. SEASONAL SENSATIONS

Halloween and Christmas are popular times of year for tourists. Fright Fest at Six Flags turns the entire park into a haunted house with live music and scary events for the whole family. Holiday in the Park is a time when the whole park becomes so lit, it becomes a winter wonderland with some of the best homemade hot cocoa. Prairie Lights is one of the largest light displays in North Texas. I have gotten to walk through Prairie Lights and loved it. They had a main house decorated with icicle lights and served hot cocoa against the cold of the nights. There were carriage rides and different shows dedicated to the multiple cultural holidays held at the same time of year. Ice at the Gaylord displays huge ice sculptures in the form of a theme every year. The New Year's Eve party is another city-wide event worth mentioning. There's so much for everyone to do!

35. LOCAL MALLS

There are many malls in Dallas and the surrounding areas. North Park and the Galleria are two of the closest malls. They have a variety of higher priced goods complete with a food court. The Galleria hosts an ice rink where couples, kids and families can go to skate. They also offer figure-skating lessons. North Park is the place closest to Dallas and has a popular attraction featuring trains for children to climb on and explore during the holidays.

36. OUTLET MALLS

Outlet malls are almost the same as the inside malls. The difference is the storefronts are outside so people could enjoy the weather. They often carry the same types of stores as inside stores varying from clothing stores to gaming and books. Some good ones to note are the Shops at Willow Bend, Fairview, and Tanger Outlet malls. These are some of my favorite places to shop. You're still outside and enjoying the fresh air and seeing other people but you can go inside the nearest store if you get too hot and need a break. The Shops at Willow Bend are always bustling during the holidays. It's a great place to meet people and build new friendships. Beware Black Fridays though. They can get crazy.

37. BEST CAMP SITES

There are a variety of Texas State Parks in the areas surrounding Dallas. Just north of it, the small town of Pilot Point houses Lake Ray Roberts State Park. It has a beautiful lakeside view and the drive isn't too far from the Metroplex. My kids and I go there during the summer when we don't want to stay stuck in the house. It's a great place to grill hot dogs and hamburgers for a picnic. The sand is perfect for sand castles or getting buried to escape the sun. Lake Ray Hubbert was one of my favorite places to fish with my uncle, sister and cousin as a child. He would wake us up really early in the morning and we would get some stink bait and go fishing for catfish. Sometimes we even brought it back to fry up in homemade batter. Lewisville is another campsite worth checking out if you're looking to enjoy the outdoors. White Rock Lake is a great place to fish and walk. We go there to do a charity walk and enjoy it every year. Somehow we always manage to score a nice breeze to combat the summer sun. One year we got caught in a storm and had to beat it back to the truck to avoid getting soaked. We didn't get there fast enough.

38. IT'S A SPEED LIMIT, NOT A SPEED SUGGESTION

Texas is a state that enforces its speed limits. Even on the back country roads, State Troopers give tickets for the smallest speeding infraction. On the toll roads, especially, police officers can be seen pulling cars over on both sides. Even if you feel like speeding, don't. Most likely an officer is right up the road, ready to pull you over and give you a ticket.

39. BE SAFE WHEN DRIVING

There are a few highways in Dallas notorious for having wrecks during the busiest times of the day. I-635 and I-35 are two of the most occupied during early morning and late work hours. Be safe and abide by the rules of the road. They could wind up saving your life. Also, don't text and drive. It is another thing to keep in mind if you want to "arrive alive" as we say in Dallas. I have witnessed many wrecks, including one my husband was in, where a cell phone was involved. It cannot be stressed enough to leave the phone alone while you're driving. To be kind, I often let the driver next to me on their phone to put it down for safety reasons. As a mom of two children, I don't want to be a casualty because someone thought it was okay to text about a party while driving.

40. TIMES TO AVOID THE ROADS

For visitors, the hours from 7-11am and 4-7pm are two of the busiest times on the roads. They can go incredibly slow and be very dangerous. If you have the time and don't have to leave early in the morning or late in the evening, try to wait. It can be better not to go at a snails' pace, especially in the summer when it can get really hot!

41. WEATHER HABITS

The weather is inconsistent. Around here we have jokes saying we honestly have no idea what the weather will do. During the summer it can be very hot. In the winter the temperatures can vary from below freezing to the low 70s in a matter of a day. Depending on the time of year, you may want to pack different varieties of clothes to cover both. We honestly never know what the weather will do around here.

42. ARLINGTON

If you have the time, be sure to check out Arlington. It's a well-known city and can be worth a look for a first time visitor. River Legacy park, The AT&T Stadium and Top O'Hill Terrace are three popular spots for a variety of people. For college students, The University of Texas at Arlington has some of the most preferred programs and degrees around. Their paleontology department has the Archosaur Site where they have unearthed multiple fossils of pre-historic sharks! I got the pleasure of digging here at one time. You actually feel like you're standing at the bottom of a lake millions of years ago. The professor walks you around and points out the different striations showing how old the rocks are and even gives you the chance to look for your own fossil.

43. LOCAL COLLEGES

For international, transferring or students seeking colleges to go to. The Metroplex is a great place to look. Community colleges like Richland, El Centro and Collin College are three good schools to look into to get a diploma. Larger colleges like Texas Women's University, The University of North Texas, UT Arlington or The University of Texas at Dallas are also close by. You can find a variety of programs and degrees for any profession!

44. THE GRASSY KNOLL

The Grassy Knoll is a historical marker in the heart of Dallas. John F. Kennedy was assassinated supposedly by Lee Harvey Oswald driving down the very road, the Knoll overlooks. It is a good site to learn about one of the most broadcasted events in Dallas' history.

45. THE KENNEDY MUSEUM

The Kennedy Museum is housed in the very same room and floor they thought one of the shooters in the Kennedy assassination was when he shot the President. It is full of video footage of the event along with commentary from police officers and FBI agents who looked into the shooting. The whole exhibit is a must see for Dallas' visitors both abroad and from another state. The Kennedy Assassination was televised in multiple venues during the 1960s. A popular theory known as the ricocheting bullet theory tells of a bullet that may have bounced through one of the occupants of the car and into the president. The facts are extraordinary!

>TOURIST

46. LEGOLAND

Legoland is located in the Grapvine Mills Mall in historic Grapevine. It is a world full of life-size and fun size Legos for children of all ages to invent and create with these popular building blocks. It also offers visitors to book parties and events so if you're in town to see a grandchild or have a child of your own, Legoland is a good place to look to let the kids play so you can relax.

47. SEA LIFE

Sea Life is a smaller version of an aquarium. It is located at the same mall right across from Legoland and offers visitors a chance to not only see various types of oceanic life but also a chance to interact with them. As with Legoland, Sea Life welcomes larger parties who wish to host birthdays and offers a chance for its patrons to watch the feeding of multiple different creatures of the mysterious deep. Big group deals and a gift shop are also available for those interested.

48. THE DALLAS WORLD AQUARIUM

The DWA, as we call it, is a much larger version of Sea Life. Located in the downtown Dallas arts district, it offers an experience one is not likely to easily forget. A variety of sea life including sharks, rays, octopi and even penguins can be found roaming in its exhibits. Aviaries housing different birds can also be seen as you walk through the winding halls and tunnels. A gift shop is also available once the tour is complete with a gift for every budget so you can remember the time you had!

49. THE ARBORETUM

The Arboretum is much like the Dallas World Aquarium. This beautiful park has a rich variety of plant and insect life for you to enjoy. In the fall, pumpkins, scarecrows and various gourds can be seen placed in gorgeous displays where you can take pictures and kids can explore the straw huts. During the winter, it is decorated in a light show that is breath-taking. If you're in town and love exotic flowers and like to take photos, the Arboretum is definitely a must-see stop on your itinerary.

>TOURIST

50. BONNIE AND CLYDE DAYS

Pilot Point is a smaller town just outside of Denton, TX just thirty minutes North of Dallas. If you come in the month of October, you can stop in at Bonnie & Clyde days. If you didn't know, this town is the home base of the nationwide notorious criminal couple, Bonnie and Clyde. Drop on in, enjoy some reenactments, see the types of cars in the 1940s and enjoy some of the cuisine in the historic square. While you're there, stop on in at the Bear Den where you can have pizza and enjoy the company of Barnum and Bailey, our local trained bears.

>TOURIST

TOP REASONS TO BOOK THIS TRIP

The Events: There is always something going on in Dallas or the neighboring cities.

Food: We have everything from barbecue to a variety of international cuisines.

Texas Tradition: No matter where you're from, the state of Texas is dipped in tradition. You merely have to travel the streets to see the wide variety of historical downtowns and markers showing Texas pride.

>TOURIST

BONUS BOOK

50 THINGS TO KNOW ABOUT PACKING LIGHT FOR TRAVEL

PACK THE RIGHT WAY EVERY TIME

AUTHOR: MANIDIPA BHATTACHARYYA

First Published in 2015 by Dr. Lisa Rusczyk. Copyright 2015. All Rights Reserved. No part of this publication may be reproduced, including scanning and photocopying, or distributed in any form or by any means, electronic or mechanical, or stored in a database or retrieval system without prior written permission from the publisher.

Disclaimer: The publisher has put forth an effort in preparing and arranging this book. The information provided herein by the author is provided "as is". Use this information at your own risk. The publisher is not a licensed doctor. Consult your doctor before engaging in any medical activities. The publisher and author disclaim any liabilities for any loss of profit or commercial or personal damages resulting from the information contained in this book.

Edited by Melanie Howthorne

ABOUT THE AUTHOR

Manidipa Bhattacharyya is a creative writer and editor, with an education in English literature and Linguistics. After working in the IT industry for seven long years she decided to call it quits and follow her heart instead. Manidipa has been ghost writing, editing, proof reading and doing secondary research services for many story tellers and article writers for about three years. She stays in Kolkata, India with her husband and a busy two year old. In her own time Manidipa enjoys travelling, photography and writing flash fiction.

Manidipa believes in travelling light and never carries anything that she couldn't haul herself on a trip. However, travelling with her child changed the scenario. She seemed to carry the entire world with her for the baby on the first two trips. But good sense prevailed and she is again working her way to becoming a light traveler, this time with a kid.

INTRODUCTION

He who would travel happily must travel light.

-Antoine de Saint-Exupéry

Travel takes you to different places from seas and mountains to deserts and much more. In your travels you get to interact with different people and their cultures. You will, however, enjoy the sights and interact positively with these new people even more, if you are travelling light.

When you travel light your mind can be free from worry about your belongings. You do not have to spend precious vacation time waiting for your luggage to arrive after a long flight. There is be no chance of your bags going missing and the best part is that you need not pay a fee for checked baggage.

People who have mastered this art of packing light will root for you to take only one carry-on, wherever you go. However, many people can find it really hard to pack light. More so if you are travelling with children. Differentiating between "must have" and "just in case" items is the starting point. There will be ample shopping avenues at your destination which are just waiting to be explored.

This book will show you 'packing' in a new 'light' – pun intended – and help you to embrace light packing practices for all of your future travels.

Off to packing!

DEDICATION

I dedicate this book to all the travel buffs that I know, who have given me great insights into the contents of their backpacks.

THE RIGHT TRAVEL GEAR

1. CHOOSE YOUR TRAVEL GEAR CAREFULLY

While selecting your travel gear, pick items that are light weight, durable and most importantly, easy to carry. There are cases with wheels so you can drag them along – these are usually on the heavy side because of the trolley. Alternatively a backpack that you can carry comfortably on your back, or even a duffel bag that you can carry easily by hand or sling across your body are also great options. Whatever you choose, one thing to keep in mind is that the luggage itself should not weigh a ton, this will give you the flexibility to bring along one extra pair of shoes if you so desire.

>TOURIST

2. CARRY THE MINIMUM NUMBER OF BAGS

Selecting light weight luggage is not everything. You need to restrict the number of bags you carry as well. One carry-on size bag is ideal for light travel. Most carriers allow one cabin baggage plus one purse, handbag or camera bag as long as it slides under the seat in front. So technically, you can carry two items of luggage without checking them in.

3. PACK ONE EXTRA BAG

Always pack one extra empty bag along with your essential items. This could be a very light weight duffel bag or even a sturdy tote bag which takes up minimal space. In the event that you end up buying a lot of souvenirs, you already have a handy bag to stuff all that into and do not have to spend time hunting for an appropriate bag.

I'm very strict with my packing and have everything in its right place. I never change a rule. I hardly use anything in the hotel room. I wheel my own wardrobe in and that's it.

Charlie Watts

CLOTHES & ACCESSORIES
4. PLAN AHEAD

Figure out in advance what you plan to do on your trip. That will help you to pick that one dress you need for the occasion. If you are going to attend a wedding then you have to carry formal wear. If not, you can ditch the gown for something lighter that will be comfortable during long walks or on the beach.

5. WEAR THAT JACKET

Remember that wearing items will not add extra luggage for your air travel. So wear that bulky jacket that you plan to carry for your trip. This saves space and can also help keep you warm during the chilly flight.

6. MIX AND MATCH

Carry clothes that can be interchangeably used to reinvent your look. Find one top that goes well with a couple of pairs of pants or skirts. Use tops, shirts and jackets wisely along with other accessories like a scarf or a stole to create a new look.

7. CHOOSE YOUR FABRIC WISELY

Stuffing clothes in cramped bags definitely takes its toll which results in wrinkles. It is best to carry wrinkle free, synthetic clothes or merino tops. This will eliminate the need for that small iron you usually bring along.

8. DITCH CLOTHES PACK UNDERWEAR

Pack more underwear and socks. These are the things that will give you a fresh feel even if you do not get a chance to wear fresh clothes. Moreover these are easy to wash and can be dried inside the hotel room itself.

9. CHOOSE DARK OVER LIGHT

While picking your clothes choose dark coloured ones. They are easy to colour coordinate and can last longer before needing a wash. Accidental food spills and dirt from the road are less visible on darker clothes.

10. WEAR YOUR JEANS

Take only one pair of Jeans with you, which you should wear on the flight. Remember to pick a pair that can be worn for sightseeing trips and is equally eloquent for dinner. You can add variety by adding light weight cargoes and chinos.

11. CARRY SMART ACCESSORIES

The right accessory can give you a fresh look even with the same old dress. An intelligent neck-piece, a couple of bright scarves, stoles or a sarong can be used in a number of ways to add variety to your clothing. These light weight beauties can double up as a nursing cover, a light blanket, beach wear, a modesty cover for visiting places of worship, and also makes for an enthralling game of peek-a-boo.

12. LEARN TO FOLD YOUR GARMENTS

Seasoned travellers all swear by rolling their clothes for compact and wrinkle free packing. Bundle packing, where you roll the clothes around a central object as if tying it up, is also a popular method of compact and wrinkle free packing. Stacking folded clothes one on top of another is a big no-no as it makes creases extreme and they are difficult to get rid of without ironing.

13. WASH YOUR DIRTY LAUNDRY

One of the ways to avoid carrying loads of clothes is to wash the clothes you carry. At some places you might get to use the laundry services or a Laundromat but if you are in a pinch, best solution is to wash them yourself. If that is the plan then carrying quick drying clothes is highly recommended, which most often also happen to be the wrinkle free variety.

14. LEAVE THOSE TOWELS BEHIND

Regular towels take up a lot of space, are heavy and take ages to dry out. If you are staying at hotels they will provide you with towels anyway. If you are travelling to a remote place, where the availability of towels look doubtful, carry a light weight travel towel of viscose material to do the job.

15. USE A COMPRESSION BAG

Compression bags are getting lots of recommendation now days from regular travellers. These are useful for saving space in your luggage when you have to pack bulky dresses. While packing for the return trip, get help from the hotel staff to arrange a vacuum cleaner.

FOOTWEAR

16. PUT ON YOUR HIKING BOOTS

If you have plans to go hiking or trekking during your trip, you will need those bulky hiking boots. The best way to carry them is to wear them on flight to save space and luggage weight. You can remove the boots once inside and be comfortable in your socks.

17. PICKING THE RIGHT SHOES

Shoes are often the bulkiest items, along with being the dainty if you are a female. They need care and take up a lot of space in your luggage. It is advisable therefore to pick shoes very carefully. If you plan to do a lot of walking and site seeing, then wearing a pair of comfortable walking shoes are a must. For more formal occasions you can carry durable, light weight flats which will not take up much space.

18. STUFF SHOES

If you happen to pack a pair of shoes, ensure you utilize their hollow insides. Tuck small items like rolled up socks or belts to save space. They will also be easy to find.

TOILETRIES

19. STASHING TOILETRIES

Carry only absolute necessities. Airline rules dictate that for one carry-on bag, liquids and gels must be in 3.4 ounce (100ml) bottles or less, and must be packed in a one quart zip-lock bag. If you are planning to stay in a hotel, the basic things will be provided for you. It's best is to buy the rest from the local market at your destination.

20. TAKE ALONG TAMPONS

Tampons are a hard to find item in a lot of countries. Figure out how many you need and pack accordingly. For longer stays you can buy them online and have them delivered to where you are staying.

21. GET PAMPERED BEFORE YOU TRAVEL

Some avid travellers suggest getting a pedicure and manicure just the day before travelling. This not only gives you a well kept look, you also save the trouble of packing nail polish. Remember, every little bit of weight reduced adds up.

ELECTRONICS
22. LUGGING ALONG ELECTRONICS

Electronics have a large role to play in our lives today. Most of us cannot imagine our lives away from our phones, laptops or tablets. However while travelling, one must consider the amount of weight these electronics add to our luggage. Thankfully smart phones come along with all the essentials tools like a camera, email access, picture editing tools and more. They are smart to the point of eliminating the need to carry multiple gadgets. Choose a smart phone that suits all your requirements and travel with the world in your palms or pocket.

23. REDUCE THE NUMBER OF CHARGERS

If you do travel with multiple electronic devices, you will have to bear the additional burden of carrying all their chargers too. Check if a single charger can be used for multiple devices. You might also consider investing in a pocket charger. These small devices support multiple devices while keeping you charged on the go.

24. TRAVEL FRIENDLY APPS

Along with smart phones come numerous apps, which are immensely helpful in our travels. You name it and you have an app for it at hand – take pictures, sharing with friends and family, torch to light dark roads, maps, checking flight/train times, find hotels and many other things. Use these smart alternatives to traditional items like books to eliminate weight and save space.

> *I get ideas about what's essential when packing my suitcase.*

-Diane von Furstenberg

TRAVELLING WITH KIDS

25. BRING ALONG THE STROLLER

Kids might enjoy walking for a while but they soon tire out and a stroller is the just the right thing for them to rest in while you continue your tour. Strollers also double duty as a luggage carrier and shopping bag holder. Remember to pick a light weight, easy to handle brand of stroller. Better yet, find out in advance if you can rent a stroller at your destination.

26. BRING ONLY ENOUGH DIAPERS FOR YOUR TRIP

Diapers take up a lot of space and add to the weight of your luggage. Therefore it is advisable to carry just enough diapers to last through the trip and a few for afterwards, till you buy fresh stock at your destination. Unless of course you are travelling to a really remote area, in which case you have no choice but to carry the load. Otherwise diapers are something you will find pretty easily.

27. TAKE ONLY A COUPLE OF TOYS

Children are easily attracted by new things in their environment. While travelling they will find numerous 'new' objects to scrutinize and play with. Packing just one favorite toy is enough, or if there is no favorite toy leave out all of them in favor of stories or imaginary games.

28. CARRY KID FRIENDLY SNACKS

Create a small snack counter in your bag to store away quick bites for those sudden hunger pangs. Depending on the child's age this could include chocolates, raisins, dry fruits, granola bars or biscuits. Also keep a bottle of water handy for your little one. These things do not add much weight and can be adjusted in a handbag or knapsack.

29. GAMES TO CARRY

Create some travel specific, imaginary games if you have slightly grown up children, like spot the attractions. Keep a coloring book and colors handy for in-flight or hotel time. Apps on your smart phone can keep the children engaged with cartoons and story books. Older children are often entertained by games available on phones or tablets. This cuts the weight of luggage down while keeping the kids entertained.

30. LET THE KIDS CARRY THEIR LOAD

A good thing is to start early sharing of responsibilities. Let your child pick a bag of his or her choice and pack it themselves. Keep tabs on what they are stuffing in their bags by asking if they will be using that item on the trip. It could start out being just an entertainment bag initially but with growing years they will learn to sort the useful from the superfluous. Children as little as four can maneuver a small trolley suitcase like a pro- their experience in pull along toys credit. If you are worried that you may be pulling it for them, you may want to start with a backpack.

31. DECIDE ON LOCATION FOR CHILDREN TO SLEEP

While on a trip you might not always get a crib at your destination, and carrying one will make life all the more difficult. Instead call ahead to see if there are any cribs or roll out beds for children. You may even put blankets on the floor. Weave them a story about camping and they will gladly sleep without any trouble.

32. GET BABY PRODUCTS DELIVERED AT YOUR DESTINATION

If you are absolutely paranoid about not getting your favourite variety of diaper or brand of baby food, check out online stores like amazon.com for services in your destination city. You can buy things online ahead of your travel and get them delivered to your hotel upon arrival.

33. FEEDING NEEDS OF YOUR INFANTS

If you are travelling with a breastfed infant, you save the trouble of carrying bottles and bottle sanitization kits. For special food, or medications, you may need to call ahead to make sure you have a refrigerator where you are staying.

34. FEEDING NEEDS OF YOUR TODDLER

With the progression from infancy to toddler, their dietary requirements too evolve. You will have to pack some snacks for travelling time. Fresh fruits and vegetables can be purchased at your destination. Most of the cities you travel to in whichever part of the world, will have baby food products and formulas, available at the local drug-store or the supermarket.

35. PICKING CLOTHES FOR YOUR BABY

Contrary to popular belief, babies can do without many changes of clothes. At the most pack 2 outfits per day. Pack mix and match type clothes for your little one as well. Pick things which are comfortable to wear and quick to dry.

36. SELECTING SHOES FOR YOUR BABY

Like outfits, kids can make do with two pairs of comfortable shoes. If you can get some water resistant shoes it will be best. To expedite drying wet shoes, you can stuff newspaper in them then wrap them with newspaper and leave them to dry overnight.

37. KEEP ONE CHANGE OF CLOTHES HANDY

Travelling with kids can be tricky. Keep a change of clothes for the kids and mum handy in your purse or tote bag. This takes a bit of space in your hand luggage but comes extremely handy in case there are any accidents or spills.

38. LEAVE BEHIND BABY ACCESSORIES

Baby accessories like their bed, bath tub, car seat, crib etc. should be left at home. Many hotels provide a crib on request, while car seats can be borrowed from friends or rented. Babies can be given a bath in the hotel sink or even in the adult bath tub with a little bit of water. If you bring a few bath toys, they can be used in the bath, pool, and out of water. They can also be sanitized easily in the sink.

39. CARRY A SMALL LOAD OF PLASTIC BAGS

With children around there are chances of a number of soiled clothes and diapers. These plastic bags help to sort the dirt from the clean inside your big bag. These are very light weight and come in handy to other carry stuff as well at times.

PACK WITH A PURPOSE

40. PACKING FOR BUSINESS TRIPS

One neutral-colored suit should suffice. It can be paired with different shirts, ties and accessories for different occasions. One pair of black suit pants could be worn with a matching jacket for the office or with a snazzy top for dinner.

41. PACKING FOR A CRUISE

Most cruises have formal dinners, and that formal dress usually takes up a lot of space. However you might find a tuxedo to rent. For women, a short black dress with multiple accessory options will do the trick.

42. PACKING FOR A LONG TRIP OVER DIFFERENT CLIMATES

The secret packing mantra for travel over multiple climates is layering. Layering traps air around your body creating insulation against the cold. The same light t-shirt that is comfortable in a warmer climate can be the innermost layer in a colder climate.

REDUCE SOME MORE WEIGHT

43. LEAVE PRECIOUS THINGS AT HOME

Things that you would hate to lose or get damaged leave them at home. Precious jewelry, expensive gadgets or dresses, could be anything. You will not require these on your trip. Leave them at home and spare the load on your mind.

44. SEND SOUVENIRS BY MAIL

If you have spent all your money on purchasing souvenirs, carrying them back in the same bag that you brought along would be difficult. Either pack everything in another bag and check it in the airport or get everything shipped to your home. Use an international carrier for a secure transit, but this could be more expensive than the checking fees at the airport.

45. AVOID CARRYING BOOKS

Books equal to weight. There are many reading apps which you can download on your smart phone or tab. Plus there are gadgets like Kindle and Nook that are thinner and lighter alternatives to your regular book.

CHECK, GET, SET, CHECK AGAIN

46. STRATEGIZE BEFORE PACKING

Create a travel list and prepare all that you think you need to carry along. Keep everything on your bed or floor before packing and then think through once again – do I really need that? Any item that meets this question can be avoided. Remove whatever you don't really need and pack the rest.

47. TEST YOUR LUGGAGE

Once you have fully packed for the trip take a test trip with your luggage. Take your bags and go to town for window shopping for an hour. If you enjoy your hour long trip it is good to go, if not, go home and reduce the load some more. Repeat this test till you hit the right weight.

48. ADD A ROLL OF DUCT TAPE

You might wonder why, when this book has been talking about reducing stuff, we're suddenly asking you to pack something totally unusual. This is because when you have limited supplies, duct tape is immensely helpful for small repairs – a broken bag, leaking zip-lock bag, broken sunglasses, you name it and duct tape can fix it, temporarily.

49. LIST OF ESSENTIAL ITEMS

Even though the emphasis is on packing light, there are things which have to be carried for any trip. Here is our list of essentials:

- Passport/Visa or any other ID

- Any other paper work that might be required on a trip like permits, hotel reservation confirmations etc.

- Medicines – all your prescription medicines and emergency kit, especially if you are travelling with children

- Medical or vaccination records

- Money in foreign currency if travelling to a different country

- Tickets- Email or Message them to your phone

50. MAKE THE MOST OF YOUR TRIP

Wherever you are going, whatever you hope to do we encourage you to embrace it whole-heartedly. Take in the scenery, the culture and above all, enjoy your time away from home.

On a long journey even a straw weighs heavy.

-Spanish Proverb

>TOURIST

PACKING AND PLANNING TIPS

A Week before Leaving

- Arrange for someone to take care of pets and water plants
- Stop mail and newspaper
- Notify Credit Card companies where you are going.
- Change your thermostat settings
- Car inspected, oil is changed, and tires have the correct pressure.
- Passports and id is up to date.
- Pay bills.
- Copy important items and download travel Apps.
- Start collecting small bills for tips

Right Before Leaving

- Clean out refrigerator.
- Empty garbage cans.
- Lock windows.
- Make sure you have the right ID with you.
- Bring cash for tips.
- Remember travel documents.
- Lock door behind you.
- Remember wallet.
- Unplug items in house and pack chargers.

READ OTHER GREATER THAN A TOURIST BOOKS

Greater Than a Tourist San Miguel de Allende Guanajuato Mexico: 50 Travel Tips from a Local by Tom Peterson

Greater Than a Tourist – Lake George Area New York USA: 50 Travel Tips from a Local by Janine Hirschklau

Greater Than a Tourist – Monterey California United States: 50 Travel Tips from a Local by Katie Begley

Greater Than a Tourist – Chanai Crete Greece: 50 Travel Tips from a Local by Dimitra Papagrigoraki

Greater Than a Tourist – The Garden Route Western Cape Province South Africa: 50 Travel Tips from a Local by Li-Anne McGregor van Aardt

Greater Than a Tourist – Sevilla Andalusia Spain: 50 Travel Tips from a Local by Gabi Gazon

Greater Than a Tourist – Kota Bharu Kelantan Malaysia: 50 Travel Tips from a Local by Aditi Shukla

Children's Book: Charlie the Cavalier Travels the World by Lisa Rusczyk

> TOURIST

Visit Greater Than a Tourist for Free Travel Tips
http://GreaterThanATourist.com

Sign up for the Greater Than a Tourist Newsletter for discount days, new books, and travel information:
http://eepurl.com/cxspyf

Follow us on Facebook for tips, images, and ideas:
https://www.facebook.com/GreaterThanATourist

Follow us on Pinterest for travel tips and ideas:
http://pinterest.com/GreaterThanATourist

Follow us on Instagram for beautiful travel images:
http://Instagram.com/GreaterThanATourist

> TOURIST

Please leave your honest review of this book on Amazon and Goodreads. Please send your feedback to GreaterThanaTourist@gmail.com as we continue to improve the series. Thank you. We appreciate your positive and constructive feedback. Thank you.

>TOURIST

METRIC CONVERSIONS

TEMPERATURE

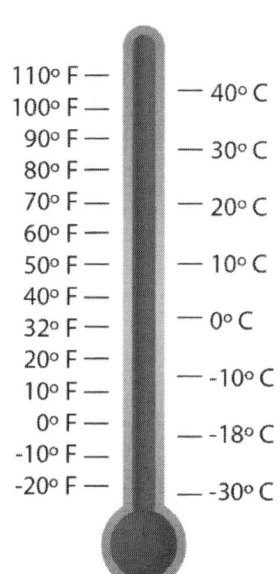

110° F — — 40° C
100° F —
90° F — — 30° C
80° F —
70° F — — 20° C
60° F —
50° F — — 10° C
40° F —
32° F — — 0° C
20° F —
10° F — — -10° C
0° F —
-10° F — — -18° C
-20° F — — -30° C

To convert F to C:
Subtract 32, and then multiply by 5/9 or .5555.

To Convert C to F:
Multiply by 1.8 and then add 32.

32F = 0C

LIQUID VOLUME

To Convert:............Multiply by
U.S. Gallons to Liters............... 3.8
U.S. Liters to Gallons 26
Imperial Gallons to U.S. Gallons 1.2
Imperial Gallons to Liters....... 4.55
Liters to Imperial Gallons 22
1 Liter = .26 U.S. Gallon
1 U.S. Gallon = 3.8 Liters

DISTANCE

To convert ....Multiply by
Inches to Centimeters 2.54
Centimeters to Inches 39
Feet to Meters....................... .3
Meters to Feet 3.28
Yards to Meters 91
Meters to Yards 1.09
Miles to Kilometers 1.61
Kilometers to Miles............ .62
1 Mile = 1.6 km
1 km = .62 Miles

WEIGHT

1 Ounce = .28 Grams
1 Pound = .4555 Kilograms
1 Gram = .04 Ounce
1 Kilogram = 2.2 Pounds

93

>TOURIST

TRAVEL QUESTIONS

- Do you bring presents home to family or friends after a vacation?
- Do you get motion sick?
- Do you have a favorite billboard?
- Do you know what to do if there is a flat tire?
- Do you like a sun roof open?
- Do you like to eat in the car?
- Do you like to wear sun glasses in the car?
- Do you like toppings on your ice cream?
- Do you use public bathrooms?
- Did you bring your cell phone and does it have power?
- Do you have a form of identification with you?
- Have you ever been pulled over by a cop?
- Have you ever given money to a stranger on a road trip?
- Have you ever taken a road trip with animals?
- Have you ever went on a vacation alone?
- Have you ever run out of gas?

- If you could move to any place in the world, where would it be?
- If you could travel anywhere in the world, where would you travel?
- If you could travel in any vehicle, which one would it be?
- If you had three things to wish for from a magic genie, what would they be?
- If you have a driver's license, how many times did it take you to pass the test?
- What are you the most afraid of on vacation?
- What do you want to get away from the most when you are on vacation?
- What foods smells bad to you?
- What item to you bring on ever trip with you away from home?
- What makes you sleepy?
- What song would you love to hear on the radio when you're cruising on the highway?
- What travel job would you want the least?
- What will you miss most while you are away from home?
- What is something you always wanted to try?

>TOURIST

- What is the best road side attraction that you ever saw?
- What is the farthest distance you ever biked?
- What is the farthest distance you ever walked?
- What is the weirdest thing you needed to buy while on vacation?
- What is your favorite candy?
- What is your favorite color car?
- What is your favorite family vacation?
- What is your favorite food in the world?
- What is your favorite gas station drink or food?
- What is your favorite license plate design?
- What is your favorite restaurant in the world?
- What is your favorite smell?
- What is your favorite song?
- What is your favorite sound that nature makes?
- What is your favorite thing to bring home from a vacation?
- What is your favorite vacation with friends?
- What is your favorite way to relax?

- What is your favorite weather conditions while driving?
- Where in the world would you rather never get to travel?
- Where is the farthest place you ever traveled in a car?
- Where is the farthest place you ever went North, South, East and West?
- Where is your favorite place in the world?
- Who is your favorite singer?
- Who taught you how to drive?
- Who will you miss the most while you are away?
- Who if the first person you will call when you get to your destination?
- Who brought you on your first vacation?
- Who likes to travel the most in your life?
- Would you rather be hot or cold?
- Would you rather drive above, below, or at the speed limited?
- Would you rather drive on a highway or a back road?
- Would you rather go on a train or a boat?
- Would you rather go to the beach or the woods?

>TOURIST
TRAVEL BUCKET LIST

>TOURIST

NOTES

Made in the USA
Middletown, DE
13 February 2025